PRESENTED TO:

FROM:

ON THE OCCASION OF:

MARY, DID YOU KNOW?

Mary, did you know that your baby boy will one day walk on water?
Mary, did you know that your baby boy will save our sons and daughters?
Did you know that your baby boy has come to make you new?
This child that you delivered will soon deliver you.

Mary, did you know that your baby boy will give sight to a blind man?
Mary, did you know that your baby boy will calm a storm with His hand?
Did you know that your baby boy has walked where angels trod?
When you kiss your little baby, you've kissed the face of God.

The blind will see, the deaf will hear, and the dead will live again.
The lame will leap, the dumb will speak the praises of the Lamb!

Mary, did you know that your baby boy is Lord of all creation?
Mary, did you know that your baby boy will one day rule the nations?
Did you know that your baby boy is heaven's perfect Lamb?
This sleeping child you're holding is the great I AM.

Mary, DID YOU KNOW?

MARK LOWRY

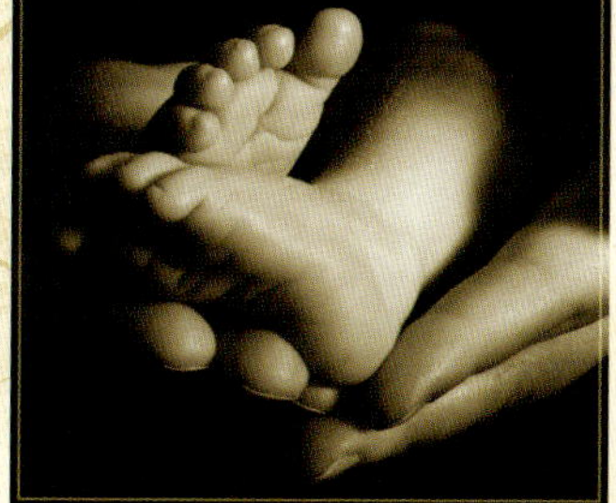

THOMAS NELSON
Since 1798

NASHVILLE MEXICO CITY RIO DE JANEIRO

Published in Nashville, Tennessee, by Thomas Nelson. Thomas Nelson is a registered trademark of HarperCollins Christian Publishing, Inc.

Managing Editor: Lisa Stilwell
Cover and interior design by Koechel Peterson Design, Minneapolis, MN.

Thomas Nelson titles may be purchased in bulk for educational, business, fund-raising, or sales promotional use. For information, please e-mail SpecialMarkets@ThomasNelson.com.

ISBN: 978-1-4041-8959-1
ISBN: 978-0-7180-3290-6 (Custom)

Printed in China

15 16 17 18 DSC 5 4 3

Foreword

Conscientious songwriters use an arsenal of well-sharpened tools to craft and deliver their intended message. Inspiration, insight, and revelation play their parts in the process, too, for when all is said and done, great songwriters know that art is greater than the sum of the parts, that the song is more than the words and the music.

But once in a while—maybe once in our lifetime if we're fortunate—there comes a song of which the writers really cannot claim ownership. The song has a sort of life of its own, and the writer was given charge of it. The writer feels more like a caretaker than an owner, and rather than sensing the need to promote the song, the writer works to protect it and keep it pure.

I think Mark Lowry and Buddy Greene would say that is true of their song, which has become the consummate incarnational song of our lifetime: "Mary, Did You Know?" The lyric came to Mark, and some good musicians made a few attempts to write music. But Mark didn't feel settled about letting the words go. One day on our bus, he showed the words to Buddy and asked if he had any ideas. Buddy studied the lyric and took it home. That week, when Buddy called and sang Mark's lyrics over the phone, something resonated in Mark's soul—and this once-in-a-lifetime song has been resonating in souls around the world ever since!

—*Gloria Gaither*

Mary, did you know

THAT YOUR BABY

BOY WILL ONE DAY

WALK ON WATER?

Mary, did you know

THAT YOUR BABY BOY
WILL SAVE OUR SONS
AND DAUGHTERS?

Think of Mary of Nazareth, called from her girlhood dreams to travel the road of a lonely destiny, to be the mother of Jesus; think of how she shrank back trembling from the call and from the sword that was to pierce her heart, until at last she bowed her head, and said, "Behold, the handmaid of the Lord."

James Stewart

I wonder if... Mary realized the power, authority, and majesty she cradled in her arms that first Christmas morning.

Blessed is the Lord God of Israel, for He has visited and redeemed His people, and has raised up a horn of salvation for us....

LUKE 1:68–69

WRAPPED IN SWADDLING CLOTHES... in an eight-pound bundle . . . gaining nourishment from her breast . . . was God. She had just given birth to the one who created her—the fullness of the godhead looking around with the wide-eyed wonder of a newborn.

God became a crying, nursing, diaper-wearing baby boy.

He seemed so tiny, wrapped tight in a long linen band and sleeping soundly like any other baby. He slept as though the world had not waited thousands of years for that moment....As though all the sin and sorrow of the world was not His concern.

Ruth Bell Graham,
One Wintry Night

They tell me every mother counts the fingers and toes of her newborn child... to make sure they're all there.

BUT I WONDER IF MARY REALIZED those tiny hands that were curled around her fingers were the same hands that had formed mankind? Those little feet were the same feet that had walked on streets of gold and been worshiped by angels. That tiny infant voice had once spoken worlds into existence.

On that first Christmas morning when she kissed her newborn child, she wasn't just kissing a baby—she was kissing the face of God.

When Mary was visited by Gabriel and told she was to have a baby—and not just a baby but *the* baby, the one every Jewish girl hoped she would be privileged to bear—she didn't ask why but rather how. She could quite understandably have asked, "Why? And why now? Why here?" Instead, she simply asked, "How?" The answer to "How can I possibly do the will of God in this incredible situation?" was quite simple, given by the angel visitor: "The Holy Spirit. . . ." Immediately Mary responded with a glad "I am the Lord's servant."

Jill Briscoe,
Heartstrings

God became one of us . . .
with our limitations.

A woman who fears the
Lord, she shall be praised.
PROVERBS 31:30

HE LEFT HIS ABILITY TO BE EVERYWHERE. He left His ability to know everything. He, like us, had to get His information from the Father. He left His throne in heaven to become a newborn baby boy. What a way for God to enter the world! Who could have devised such a plan . . . but God?

Did you know

THAT YOUR BABY BOY HAS
COME TO MAKE YOU NEW?

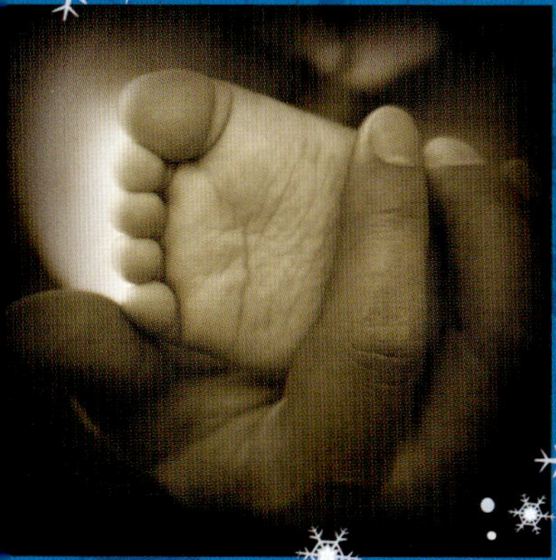

THIS CHILD

THAT YOU DELIVERED

WILL SOON DELIVER YOU.

Jesus came to fulfill the law— because we couldn't.

And the only way He could fulfill the law was to become one of us. But how can you fulfill the law if it doesn't apply to you? How could God fulfill the law? It doesn't apply to Him. How could God covet His neighbor's wife? Who is God going to steal from? He owns it all!

The only way He could fulfill the law was to become one of us.

By the incarnation, God broke His silence.

—IGNATIUS

TO BE TEMPTED JUST LIKE US...
but to say "no" to the temptation. Then,
after saying "no" for thirty-three years,
He drank the cup,
became our sin,
took our beating,
died in our place,
and rose from the dead.

But I'm getting ahead of myself. What did Mary know?

And she brought forth her firstborn Son, and wrapped Him in swaddling cloths, and laid Him in a manger, because there was no room for them in the inn.

LUKE 2:7

MARY HAD RECEIVED HER INFORMATION FROM AN ANGEL (a messenger sent by God).

"Mary, you have nothing to fear. God has a surprise for you: You will become pregnant and give birth to a son and call His name Jesus. He will be great. He will be called 'Son of the Highest.' The Lord God will give him the throne of his father David; He will rule Jacob's house forever—there will be no end, ever, to his kingdom" (Luke 1:29, MSG).

Hush, my babe; be still and slumber,
Holy angels guard thy bed,
Heavenly blessings without number
Gently resting on thy head.

Laura Ingalls Wilder

The Advent message is that one homeless night long ago, in a place called Bethlehem, God wrapped humanity's broken songs and shattered chords with the music of the spheres.

Leonard Sweet

Unto us a Child is born,
Unto us a Son is given;
And the government will be upon His shoulder.
And His name will be called
Wonderful, Counselor, Mighty God,
Everlasting Father, Prince of Peace.
Of the increase of His government and peace
There will be no end.

ISAIAH 9:6–7

That's all the information she had.

Sounds like a good deal.

Her son's gonna be king.

But did she know about the beatings?

Did she know about Gethsemane?

Did she know about the cross?

Did she know about the resurrection?

I don't think so. Aren't you glad God gives us just enough light to take the next step? He doesn't tell us everything that lies ahead. He gives us just enough information to spark our interest, to encourage us to follow. And the life-changing events He keeps to Himself…until we're ready for them.

Mary, did you know

THAT YOUR BABY BOY
WILL GIVE SIGHT TO
A BLIND MAN?

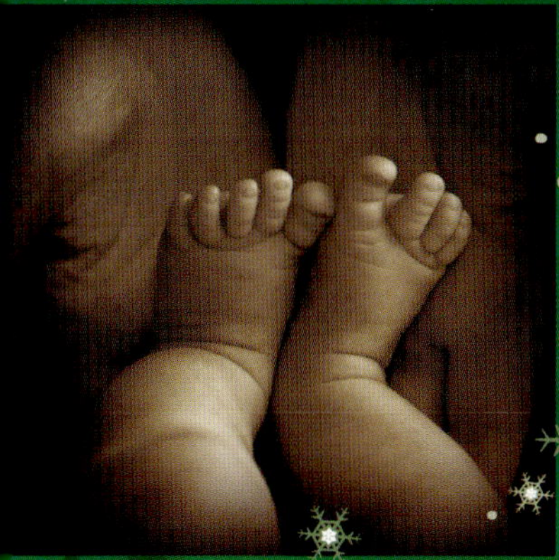

Mary, did you know

THAT YOUR BABY BOY
WILL CALM A STORM
WITH HIS HAND?

Mary, grasped and seized by the Spirit, speaks of God's coming into the world, of the advent of Jesus Christ. For she knows better than anyone what it means to wait for Christ.

She waits for Him in a way unlike anyone else. She awaits Him as His mother. She knows about the mystery of His coming, about the Spirit that is at play here, about the almighty God who works His wonders.

She experiences in her own body that God's ways with humans are wonderful, that He isn't bound by human standards, that He doesn't follow the path that humans like to lay out for Him—that His way is beyond all understanding, beyond all proof, free, and with a mind of its own.

Dietrich Bonhoeffer,
The Mystery of Holy Night

Behold! The Lamb of God who takes away the sin of the world!

JOHN 1:29

I don't know how much Mary knew. But I do know she knew an angel had come to her.

AND THAT ANGEL *had told her, "The Holy Spirit will come upon you, and the power of the Highest overshadow you; therefore, also the Holy One who is to be born will be called the Son of God"* (Luke 1:35).

The Lord gives us signs and landmarks on our journey. The virgin birth was the perfect landmark in Mary's life. If anyone KNEW Jesus was virgin-born…she knew it. That's one thing she would never doubt. And God knew she would need very strong landmarks. She was walking down a road no one had ever walked before. She was the virgin whom Isaiah had prophesied would deliver the Messiah to the world.

But as Mary's stomach grew, neighbors stared. An angel came to Joseph, who believed and took Mary to be his wife.

The hinge of history is on the door of a Bethlehem stable.

Lucille Sollenberger

I've always loved the smell of barns and farms and animals and such.

I WAS A WEIRD KID. I think I loved that special aroma because I was raised in the city. Visiting a friend's farm was a rare and special event. The smell of barnyard animals didn't represent sweat and work to me. It represented special weekend outings.

Who among us will celebrate Christmas right?
Those who finally lay down all their power, honor, and prestige
all their vanity, pride, and self-will at the manger,
those who stand by the lowly and let God alone be exalted,
those who see in the child in the manger the glory of God
precisely in this lowliness.

Dietrich Bonhoeffer,
The Mystery of Holy Night

I think that because of my "big city upbringing" and the beautiful Christmas cards I've seen through the years, I've had a fairytale idea of what it was like in the stable that first Christmas night.

Mary kept all these things and pondered them in her heart.

LUKE 2:19

I'VE ALWAYS PICTURED MARY in her "blue Mary outfit" with the angelic halo around her head, the animals standing in silent reverence, Joseph beside Mary, and the shepherds kneeling in front of the newborn child.

Did you know

THAT YOUR BABY BOY
HAS WALKED WHERE
ANGELS TROD?

When you

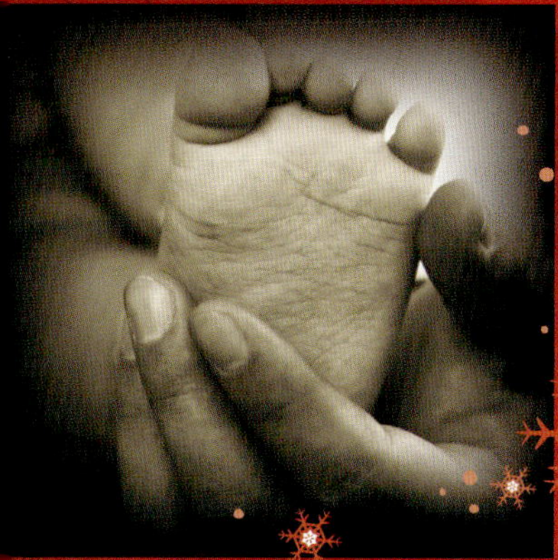

kiss your little baby,

YOU'VE KISSED THE FACE OF GOD.

Who remembers small-town Christmas Eves that were always celebrated with a pageant at the church? And the snow that fell so softly, as whole families headed toward this focal point....

Garbed in bathrobes and turbaned in towels, your father and other men became strangers saying, "Let us go now even unto Bethlehem and see this thing which has come to pass." And the click and swish of the sheets being pulled. And at last the revelation: for there stood Joseph beside a manger with real straw. And Mary cradling a baby—sometimes a big doll, but once a real baby. The minister's new baby! You could hear it crowing and glimpse a moving hand. It lived! For a breathless, rapturous moment, the living breathing Christ child was right there in your midst.

Marjorie Holmes
Love and Laughter

But I doubt that's the way it really was.

Suddenly there was with the angel a multitude of the heavenly host praising God and saying:
"Glory to God in the highest,
And on earth peace, goodwill toward men!"

LUKE 2:13–14

MARY HAD TO DELIVER HER FIRSTBORN into the world with as much straining, blood, and afterbirth as the rest of the women who had given birth before her. She didn't have the luxury of an epidural, heart monitoring machines, and forceps. There were only a few barn animals and her husband Joseph to witness the birth of God.

I'll tell you whom I feel sorry for—
all the people in the inn who missed it.
They were there!

THEY WERE IN THE SAME TIME PERIOD. They didn't have to learn of this event 2,000 years after the fact, like we did. While they were lying in their beds, trying to get some rest . . . they missed it! They could have walked right out to the stable and witnessed the coming of the Messiah! . . . But they were too busy with the mundane to notice the eternal.

LOOK, MARY, LOOK

Mary look, the baby's smiling—
Hearing Joseph call His name!
Isn't this the confirmation
Of that which the angel claimed?
Yes, your baby's in a manger;
Lying in a dirty stall.
Look again—He's Son of David;
King of Jacob; Lord of all.

Mary look, it's Joseph crying—
Worshipping the son you bore.
What a husband there beside you,
Kneeling humbly on the floor!
Tiny babe holds calloused finger;
Something touching deeply there.
God indeed is in the stable—
Granting vision; bringing care.

Mary look, the shepherds coming—
Calling out to greet their King!
Do you know the proclamation
That they heard the angels bring?
"You will find Him in a manger;
Wrapped and lying in the straw"
Mary, you are not in danger,
Look how God prescribed it all.

Mary look, the star appearing!
Moving higher into view!
What a strange, but precious wonder,
There abiding over you.
See, the star shines into heaven—
Angels' mark where God met man!
Hidden from the view of mortals,
God completes what He began.

Look, Mary, look,
It wasn't just a dream.
God's indeed at work,
Despite how things might seem.

Kevin Hartnett

Salvation is God-given, God-driven, God-empowered, and God-originated. The gift is not from man to God. It is from God to man.

Max Lucado

My dad believes Jesus knew who He was the second He was conceived.

Joseph and his mother marveled at those things which were spoken of Him.

LUKE 2:33

I TOLD MY DAD, "Then He was faking all those diaper changes." How did Jesus learn who He was? Did He learn from His mother's bed-time stories? Her stories must have been full of wise men, angels, and stars in the sky. Did Jesus ever crawl up in Mary's lap and say, "Mama, tell me the one about the angel again. What did he say to you that night?" or, "Mama, tell me the story of the wise men who brought those gifts."

The blind will see,

THE DEAF WILL HEAR,

the dead will live again.

THE LAME WILL LEAP,

the dumb will speak

THE PRAISES OF THE LAMB!

We never knew how hungry we were for God until Jesus arrived. When He was delivered onto the stable straw, we caught the fragrance of the presence of God. We inhaled the aroma of "God with us" and became acutely aware of a hunger deep inside. We hardly had words for it, but it was . . . it *is* a longing for the Lord.

Joni Eareckson Tada,
A Christmas Longing

Then Simeon . . . said to Mary His mother, "Behold, this Child is destined for the fall and rising of many in Israel, and for a sign which will be spoken against (yes, a sword will pierce through your own soul also), that the thoughts of many hearts may be revealed."

LUKE 2:34–35

As He studied the Scriptures He must have seen His face on every page... because His life was fulfilling every prophecy.

I BELIEVE JESUS KNEW WHO HE WAS by the time He was twelve. He ditched His mother for two days. (That's when I knew I wanted to be a Christian, ... when I found out that God ditched His mom.) Mary left Jerusalem with her family and the rest of the crowd. She thought Jesus was with them. But Jesus had stayed behind to confuse and confound the elders of the temple with His knowledge and questions.

Can you imagine the panic in Mary's heart when she realized Jesus wasn't with them?

Sing, O heavens!
Be joyful, O earth!
And break out in
singing, O mountains!
For the LORD *has*
comforted His people,
And will have mercy
on His afflicted.

ISAIAH 49:13

SHE HAD BEEN ENTRUSTED WITH GOD'S CHILD—and she had lost Him!

She raced back to Jerusalem to find Jesus teaching in the temple. She started to scold Him. "Where have You been? We've been worried sick about You."

Don't miracles manifest themselves in the darkest shadows? When it seems light will never find its way through a storm of agonies, there appears a golden ray like dawn across the otherwise hopelessly bleak landscape. Jesus came to earth so we can sing and laugh, no matter what storm we're up against.

Marie Chapian

Jesus said, "Don't you know I must be about My Father's business?"

AND SHE BOUGHT IT! That line never worked for me. I tried it. I didn't get away with it. My mother knew I wasn't virgin-born. But Mary knew Jesus was... and that He must be about His Father's business. I believe He was saying, *Don't you know? Aren't you the one who told me? Don't you remember the bedtime stories? Have you forgotten the angel?... I must be about My Father's business.*

Then there are the silent years in the life of Christ. Between age twelve and thirty, we don't know what happened.

BUT IT MAKES YOU WONDER. Did Jesus ever perform any miracles around the house? He must have. Otherwise, how would Mary know that He could turn water into wine? And they must have had *many* discussions about when He would begin His public ministry, because when He was thirty He was still living at home!

Mary, did you know

THAT YOUR BABY BOY IS
LORD OF ALL CREATION?

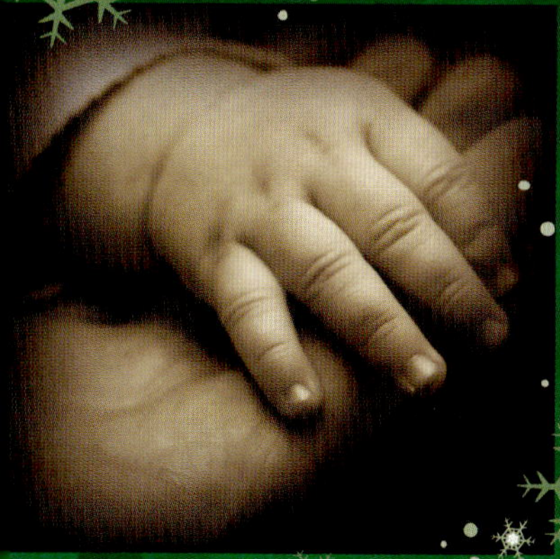

Mary, did you know

THAT YOUR BABY BOY

WILL ONE DAY RULE

THE NATIONS?

I was only seven years old, but from then on, it was clear that December 25 was a special day. A holy day. The candle-light Christmas Eve service at our Reformed Episcopal Church had new and deeper meaning....

The sanctuary was dark, but oh, so warm. Up and down each pew a candle was passed to light the one we held in our hands. When mine was lit, I held it tightly, staring into the flame. I felt as though I were holding something holy. When I leaned on the kneelers to pray, I tried to make my prayer last as long as the little candle, as though that would be proof of my heart's desire that this be an important night. I wanted Jesus to know how special I thought He was.

Joni Eareckson Tada,
A Christmas Longing

Can a woman forget her nursing child and not have compassion on the son of her womb?

ISAIAH 49:15

Mary knows Jesus is the Messiah.

JESUS KNOWS HE IS THE MESSIAH. And she walks up to Him in front of some servants at a marriage supper and says, "They've run out of wine at the marriage supper."

Has your mother ever said something to you . . . you hear what she says . . . but you know what she *means*? I believe this was one of those times for Jesus. His mother simply said, "They've run out of wine at the marriage supper." Then He gave that strange response, "Woman, what have I to do with thee? It's not my time." Time for what? If my mother had said to me, "They've run out of Diet Coke at the party," I wouldn't think she wanted me to turn water into Diet Coke. I would think she wanted me to go down to the grocery store and get some more Diet Coke! But Jesus' reaction leads me to believe they had had this discussion before. And even though Jesus didn't realize it was His time to start performing miracles, somehow *she* knew. Because even though He said "It's not My time," . . . in actuality, it was!

Now the eastern star
Shines from afar
To light the poorest home;
Hearts warmer grow,
Gifts freely flow,
For Christmas-tide has come.

Louisa May Alcott

Let this mind be in you which was also in Christ Jesus, who, being in the form of God, did not consider it robbery to be equal with God, but made Himself of no reputation, taking the form of a bondservant, and coming in the likeness of men.

PHILIPPIANS 2:5–7

Turning water into wine was just the beginning. From that moment on, Jesus began performing many miracles.

He gave sight to the blind,
a new mind to the demon-possessed,
legs to the lame,
a fresh start to the leper,
and to all who would really listen . . . a new life.

HE HAS COME! He may really be seen, beheld! He is the promised One who would give the solution to the broken spoiled world. The lambs used in worship by Abraham, Moses, and all through history, looked forward to *the* Lamb. And now—here He is. Shivers of fearful and delightful recognition should fill you and go up and down your spine. To take this with a flat, dry, dusty, theological kind of attitude, whether positive of negative, is horrible!

Behold the Lamb of God!

Edith Schaeffer,
Forever Music

And Mary saw it all.

JESUS NEVER TRAVELED MORE than thirty miles from His birthplace. I'm sure she was there for the baptism, the feeding of the thousands with a little boy's lunch, and every other major event of His life.

Did you know

THAT YOUR BABY BOY IS
HEAVEN'S PERFECT LAMB?

This sleeping

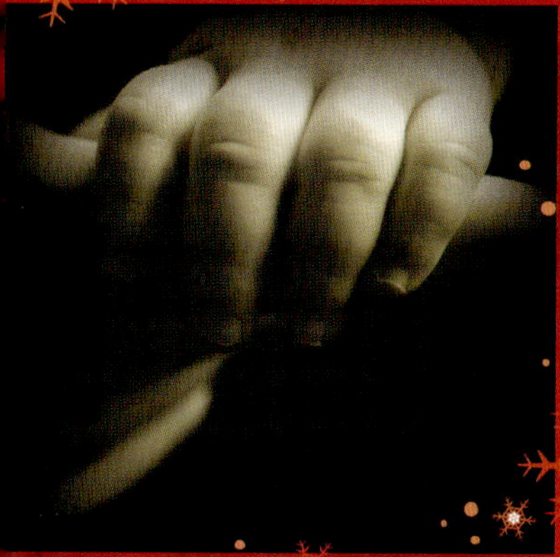

child you're holding

IS THE GREAT I AM.

Angels we have heard on high
Singing sweetly through the night,
And the mountains in reply
Echoing their brave delight.

French Christmas Carol

And she was there when they crucified Him. Most of the others had scattered like the wind.

PETER WAS WARMING HIMSELF BY A FIRE, denying he even knew Jesus. But Mary was there. That was her firstborn hanging on the cross.

She had nursed Him.

She had changed His diapers.

She had watched Him learn to crawl and then walk.

She had told Him bedtime stories.

She had rocked Him and calmed His fears at night.

And Mary said:

"My soul magnifies the Lord,
And my spirit has rejoiced in God my Savior.
For He has regarded the lowly state of His maidservant;
For behold, henceforth all generations will call me blessed.
For He who is mighty has done great things for me,
And holy is His name.
And His mercy is on those who fear Him
From generation to generation.
He has shown strength with His arm;
He has scattered the proud in the imagination of their hearts.
He has put down the mighty from their thrones,
And exalted the lowly.
He has filled the hungry with good things,
And the rich He has sent away empty.
He has helped His servant Israel,
In remembrance of His mercy,
As He spoke to our fathers,
To Abraham and to his seed forever."

LUKE 1:46–55

James and Jude, the half-brothers of Jesus, were nowhere to be found.

In fact, they didn't even believe in Jesus as Savior until after the Resurrection. (It would be hard to acknowledge that your older brother was not just *good*. . . He was *God!*)

But Mary saw it all. She was the first one to hold Him when He entered the world, and she was the last one to hold Him at the end of His life.

As the year draws to a close, Christmas offers its wonderful message. Emmanuel. God with us. He who resided in heaven, co-equal and co-eternal with the Father and the Spirit, willingly descended into our world. He breathed our air, felt our pain, knew our sorrows, and died for our sins. He didn't come to frighten us, but to show us the way to warmth and safety.

Charles Swindoll,
The Finishing Touch

Mary saw it all.
The Birth.
The Life.
The Death.

Praise the L*ORD!*

Praise God in His sanctuary;

Praise Him in His mighty firmament!

Praise Him for His mighty acts;

Praise Him according to His excellent greatness!

Let everything that has breath praise the L*ORD!*

PSALM 150:1, 2, 6

And Mary was there to see Him after the Resurrection.

And it came to pass in those days that a decree went out from Caesar Augustus that all the world should be registered. This census first took place while Quirinius was governing Syria. So all went to be registered, everyone to his own city.

Joseph also went up from Galilee, out of the city of Nazareth, into Judea, to the city of David, which is called Bethlehem, because he was of the house and lineage of David, to be registered with Mary, his betrothed wife, who was with child. So it was, that while they were there, the days were completed for her to be delivered. And she brought forth her firstborn Son, and wrapped Him in swaddling cloths, and laid Him in a manger, because there was no room for them in the inn.

LUKE 2:1–7

Jesus never asked us to remember His birth.

Look to Me, and be saved,
All you ends of the earth!
For I am God, and there
is no other.

ISAIAH 45:22

He asked us to remember His death, because through His death we have found life. By believing in the Lord Jesus Christ, we are saved.

Peter had to believe for himself. Thomas had to believe for himself. James and Jude had to believe for themselves. Mary, the mother of Jesus, also needed a savior. She had to believe for herself. And because we have chosen to believe in the virgin-born, crucified and risen Savior, Jesus Christ, we know we have received eternal life.

And this, for sure, Mary knew.

Acknowledgments

Grateful acknowledgment is made to the following publishers and copyright holders for permission to reprint copyrighted material:

RUTH BELL GRAHAM, *One Wintry Night.*
Grand Rapids, MI: Baker Book House, 2007. © Ruth Bell Graham.

JILL BRISCOE, *Heartstrings: Finding a Song When You've Lost Your Joy.*
Wheaton, IL: Tyndale House, © 1997.

DIETRICH BONHOEFFER, *The Mystery of Holy Night.*
New York: Crossroad Publishing, © 1997.

MARJORIE HOLMES, *Love and Laughter.*
New York: Bantam Doubleday Dell. © 1967 Marjorie Holmes.

KEVIN HARTNETT, "Look Mary Look."
© 2006 Kevin Hartnett. KHartnettPoetry.typepad.com.
Used with permission.

JONI EARECKSON TADA, *A Christmas Longing.*
Sisters, OR: Multnomah Books, © 1990.

EDITH SCHAEFFER, *Forever Music.*
Nashville, TN: Thomas Nelson. © 1986 Edith Schaeffer.

CHARLES SWINDOLL, *The Finishing Touch.*
Nashville, TN: Thomas Nelson. © 1994 Charles Swindoll.